# STORIES TO DRAW

by

## JERRY J. MALLETT

and

## MARIAN R. BARTCH

**FRELINE, INC.**
Hagerstown, Maryland
1982

FRELINE, INC.
P.O. Box 889
Hagerstown, Maryland 21740

Library of Congress Cataloging in Publication Data

Mallett, Jerry J., 1939-
    Stories to draw.

    1. Story-telling. 2. Chalk-talks. I. Bartch, Marian R.
II. Title.
Z718.3.M26          027.62'5          82-2399
ISBN 0-913853-00-3                    AACR2

This book is dedicated to . . .

Carla, who loves stories.

mrb


and


John and Maude Brown, who filled my
childhood with many stories.

jjm

# FOREWORD

*Stories To Draw* provides librarians and teachers with a variety of easy-to-learn and fun-to-use stories for children. Each story can be told or read to youngsters . . . while at the same time the storyteller draws simple lines on a chalkboard or posterboard to illustrate the story. Each story becomes extra special as children see the story and picture unfold together.

The goal of the authors is to provide a variety of amusing chalk talk stories to interest and entertain children and to give suggestions for rehearsing them to ensure storytelling success. Both the novice and experienced storyteller will find these chalk talk stories enjoyable to prepare and share with children.

The authors recommend that readers follow five steps in using this book. First, read "About Storytelling;" second, select your favorites from among the many chalk talks found in *Stories To Draw*; third, practice the story or stories you plan to present; fourth, present your chalk talks to delight and amuse children; fifth, encourage children to create and present their own chalk talks.

*Stories To Draw* will "open doors" to many new and enjoyable storytelling experiences. You are cordially invited to "walk in" and join the fun.

# TABLE OF CONTENTS

# ABOUT STORYTELLING

## The Value of Storytelling

Historically, storytelling has been of significant value in perpetuating the cultural and moral development of society. Centuries ago the tribal storyteller was considered a person of great importance and was depended on for entertainment, relaxation, and enlightenment. His stories lifted the human spirit, helped people share their hopes and dreams, and gave them a sense of closeness and belonging.

Although in today's culture we no longer have "tribal" storytellers, the heritage of their contributions remains. The satisfactions shared by ancient peoples are fundamentally the same as those we enjoy today when we hear enthusiastic and accomplished storytellers weave their magic.

Storytelling needs special emphasis in the modern classroom or library so that these same benefits and satisfactions can be shared with all students. Through storytelling both the listener and the storyteller can develop a greater appreciation for literature, drama, and oral communication.

There are added advantages when storytelling is integrated into one's everyday classroom routine. A teacher or librarian who takes the time and effort to select, learn, and effectively present a story to the class communicates not only a caring for good literature, but also a caring for the members of the class.

Sharing a story can be an intimate and personal experience for the storyteller and the listeners. Storytellers share something of themselves with the telling of each story, and listeners reciprocate in the process through their responses. This two-way communication can build a classroom atmosphere of mutual trust, caring and warmth, helping a class to become a more cohesive group.

Telling a story in contrast to reading it can have other advantages. First, there is no barrier between you, the storyteller, and your audience. With no book in hand you can more easily establish and maintain direct eye contact with your listeners. Being able to concentrate on the faces, attitudes, and postures of listeners permits you to more easily "read" their responses. This feedback can signal when a word or phrase needs explaining, when the tempo of telling needs to be slower or faster, or when the length of your story needs cutting. In addition, the creative and imaginative powers of children can be brought into full play when you help them form "mind pictures" from your spoken word-pictures.

Telling stories is an active, dynamic process which provides you with an added dimension to personal communication and increases your understanding and awareness of your listeners and their needs. Much of your enjoyment in storytelling will be received by watching the interested and enthusiastic responses of your listeners. This is highly satisfying, rewarding, and worth all the extra time and effort involved in preparing a story. Listeners will cherish and remember the happy times you spend telling them stories. Storytelling is indeed special and time well-spent, whatever the setting.

## The Place of Storytelling in the Classroom or Library

Storytelling is a highly specialized art form in which anyone with a genuine desire to communicate with others can excel. Your classroom or library is a perfect setting for the development and expression of your storytelling ability. Most teachers and librarians will recognize opportunities for enriching studies of subject matter through the use of well-timed and well-told stories. Stories can greatly reinforce learning and help with recall of what is being taught. You need only explore resource material available in this book in order to take advantage of your talents and the situation. Your class provides a ready-made audience eager to hear your story unfold. When well told, your stories will hold listeners in rapt attention.

Even if you feel unsure of your storytelling ability, you may have unrecognized experience to draw on. Perhaps your experience has been of an informal nature, such as telling a joke to a friend, rather than formal, as before a large group. Perhaps you have had experience more as a responder than as a teller, but the experience has taken place. A few sessions of storytelling . . . especially with *Stories To Draw* . . . will be enough to convince you what a pleasant and beneficial experience storytelling can be.

## Where to Begin . . . The Chalk Talk

A very special storytelling technique, one that holds great fascination for listeners, is that of the chalk talk . . . and that's what this book is all about. The chalk talk is an excellent and easy method useful for both the beginning and veteran storyteller. A story's sequence of action is revealed on the chalkboard (or on a large piece of posterboard if no chalkboard is available) through connecting lines and shapes which develop toward the culmination of the story. The finished drawing makes the point of the story . . . often in a surprising or humorous way. Even if you have minimal artistic talent, you can achieve immediate and gratifying success when using a chalk talk.

Knowing what the completed drawing will look like is the equivalent of having cue cards. Remembering the story will be relatively easy. The use of such a visual aid acts as an attention-holder, expanding and extending the word-pictures drawn. Chalk talks generate a great deal of excitement and pleasure as watcher-listeners relate your spoken words to the drawing taking shape on the board. Added impact is created when the drawing and story end together, right before the listener's eyes, in a marvelous totality of an often unexpected climax.

## The Preparation Process

Preparing a chalk talk involves the same steps necessary in preparing any other kind of story, but with a few additional considerations. Certain guidelines should be followed carefully during the preparation process.

First, choose stories with care. Some stories in this book are better for telling than others. Some will require the use of exact words, making the task of learning the story more difficult. This kind of story should be read rather than told.

Second, to ensure full understanding, stories with the simplest illustrations are better for telling, while those with more involved drawings are better read.

Third, stories chosen should be liked and enjoyed by the teller, or the whole effort will lack effectiveness. It is hard to feign enthusiasm for a story, and if the storyteller is not enjoying it, neither will the audience.

Finally, each story used must fit the needs, ages, backgrounds, interests, and comprehension levels of the intended audience.

Assuming these factors have been considered and an appropriate story has been chosen, the next step is to learn the story. There are many ways to approach the learning process, for each of us has a unique learning style. Experimentation to find the best personal method will bring about the best results. Generally, making a list of events or sequencing is helpful. It fixes the flow of action in the teller's mind. Paraphrasing the text works much better than rote memorization, for it puts the emphasis upon the movement of the plot. The memorization of a string of words, each dependent upon the other for recall, can cause the complete loss of the story if a word or phrase is forgotten. Most effective storytellers practice (and practice and practice!) telling a story until they feel at ease and sure of themselves in remembering it. Many use a tape recorder to evaluate their presentation for pitch, enunciation, timing, and expression.

The chalk talk, of course, must also be drawn as the words are being learned. Often, starting with the finished drawing and working backwards is helpful. Having the entire drawing to work with is immensely useful in this first learning step. Practice on a chalkboard or posterboard, whichever you will be using. If possible, use a video recorder to evaluate your position at the board. It is necessary that all the listeners be able to see what is being drawn, so the teller must be careful not to block the view. If a video recorder is not available, a full-length mirror may act as a substitute.

## Time and Space

You alone must determine the proper time for telling a story, any kind of a story. Some teachers use their storytelling time as an effective tool for settling a class down just before or after recess or lunch, or at the close of the day. Others feel a story helps relax the class and makes an enjoyable break between difficult and demanding curricular tasks. Stories can also be incorporated into subject matter lesson plans in such areas as language arts, reading, social studies, even mathematics and science, to further develop interpretative, observational, and sequential skills, as well as oral and written skills.

In order to make storytelling time more special, there should be a variation from usual seating arrangements. Ideally, one corner of the room covered with some carpeting and relaxed seating provides this emphasis. If space limitations prohibit using a different part of the room, rearrange chairs in a semi-circle. If chairs and desks cannot be moved, then desk tops should be cleared of any and all kinds of distracting materials. In good weather a peaceful spot out-of-doors adds to the fun of a story . . . but it should be free of loud, unnerving noises from traffic or the playground. Whatever arrangements are made, let them communicate to your class that you feel storytelling time is special and important.

## After the Story--Student Follow-Up Activities

Many follow-up activities naturally develop from the presentation of a chalkboard story, permitting an almost effortless way to reinforce various skill areas. Immediately following the story and while the drawing is still on the board, ask the class to recall separate events of the story, remembering details and the importance of each line or shape in the drawing. This activity reinforces recall and memory skills.

Another approach is to have children individually try to list the sequence of events in the story with the visual aid of the drawing. After individual lists have been made, a group comparison can be done with the teacher listing the proper sequence on the board. Once the sequence is correctly listed, the drawing can be erased and the story retold. These activities serve to strengthen sequencing and observational skills.

Once the class has become thoroughly familiar with the chalk talk format, they can be encouraged to create an original chalk talk story. For this purpose, the class may be divided into three or four small groups to generate ideas. Then one idea can be chosen and worked on by the entire class. The teacher or librarian should be prepared to offer suggestions and ideas at this point to prevent any "bogging down" of the process. After a class story has been composed, individual class members may wish to create their own stories for presentation to the class, but this should be a voluntary activity. All that the teacher needs to provide is a piece of chalk or crayon, some drawing materials, space, and lots of positive support and encouragement to get the class going. The child's appreciation for this storytelling form will be doubly increased as he or she gains a first-hand knowledge of all that must be considered in the creation and execution of a chalk talk story.

All who wish should be given the opportunity to present a chalk talk (original or not) before the class or before a small group. Even many shy children will feel comfortable using this technique, for the major focus will be on the emerging picture rather than on the child. Chalk talks are just as effective in relaxing the teller as they are in absorbing the audience. Everyone will enjoy them.

The chalk talks which follow will provide a foundation for getting started on a fascinating art form to add interest and fun to your classroom or library story hour sessions.

# CIRCUS TIME

It was morning, and Debbie was wide awake.

"Kim, Kim," she called to her sleeping sister. "Wake up. Today's the day for the circus!"

Neither of the girls had ever been to a circus before, and today was the big day they'd been waiting for . . . when the circus came to town.

They dressed in a hurry and rushed downstairs.

"Easy does it, girls" said their mother when she saw how excited they were.

"Remember," added their father," it doesn't start until this afternoon."

To Debbie and Kim it seemed like forever before afternoon came. At last they all finished their lunch, piled into their car, and drove to the huge field where the "big top" tent had been pitched.

Soon they had bought tickets and found their seats in the grandstand. The show was about to begin.

"Look, Debbie," said Kim. "The THREE CIRCUS RINGS are arranged to form a triangle."

"I see," said Debbie. "Do you think there will be a different act in each one?"

"I don't know," laughed Kim, "but I hope not. Otherwise I won't know which way to look."

Just then the band began to play and a tall MAN in a red and blue striped costume ran into the first ring and began juggling balls, hats, and long flashing swords.

The girls were astonished when he even juggled with a blindfold over his eyes . . . and he didn't drop a thing!

After watching awhile, Debbie's attention was attracted to the second ring. She could hardly believe what she saw. A huge brown BEAR was riding a blue motorcycle and waving to the crowd.

"Kim," gasped Debbie. "Did you ever see anything more amazing?"

But before Kim could answer, the drums began to roll, and a bright SPOTLIGHT glared down from the top of the tent.

In the center of the spotlight were a man and woman dressed in spark-ily costumes. Back and forth they glided on a swinging TRAPEZE.

"Oh, how scary," whispered Kim. "Look how high up they are. I'm sure glad they have a NET under them."

"Yes," said Debbie, "but I wouldn't do that if I had ten nets under me!"
Suddenly there was a loud roar that sent chills up and down their spines. As they watched, a group of men ran out and put up a large steel CAGE around the whole performing area.

When they finished, eight wild, roaring lions came running into the cage. They perched on high stools arranged in a circle. Surrounded by these fierce beasts was a little man in a white suit who walked back and forth among them. He carried a chair, a whip, and a pistol which he used to make the lions perform their tricks.

For the last amazing trick of his act, the little man stuck his whole head between the jaws of the largest lion in the ring.

The girls were so worried they could hardly breathe. Then the act was over, and everyone cheered for the little man and his lions.

"He certainly was brave," said Debbie. "What if that huge lion had been hungry?"

"Yes," said Kim, "or what if all the lions had gotten loose and had run into the crowd!"

The girls thought nothing could top the lion act, but the band began to play again, and the Ringmaster stepped forward.

"And now, ladies and gentlemen," he said, "prepare to see the most thrilling, the most daring, the most death-defying act ever performed. Emmet and Osgood are going to dive from their high, high platforms in-to this small, small POOL of water you see here below them."

"Please be very quiet now and let them concentrate!"

Debbie and Kim looked up and saw two daring men climbing up, up, up, up, up small rope ladders attached to TWO PLATFORMS almost at the top of the tent.

"Oh, no," shuddered Debbie, "they'll never make it. I can't look."

She closed her eyes as soon as the men dived and didn't open them until she heard a loud SPLASH.

Then everyone clapped. Both men were safe, but very, very wet.

There was only one more act left, one that ended the circus show and made Debbie and Kim and everybody else laugh and laugh.

Can you guess what it was?

# BERNARD, THE DAREDEVIL BEE

All the bees in the hive knew who Bernard was. They were constantly buzzing about his strange actions. Every day one could hear them say, "Guess what Bernard's done now!" or "I just can't believe Bernard! He'll do anything!" or "Nothing he does can surprise me anymore!" Bernard was the most adventuresome of all the young bees, and even though he lived in a very fine hive, he was never satisfied to stay in it. Not Bernard! He was always looking for new excitement.

One morning Bernard looked up and saw THREE BIRDS flying way, way up in the sky.

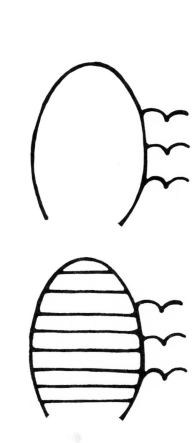

"That sure looks like fun," he thought to himself. "I'll bet I could see the whole world from up there!"

Bernard hovered in the air a few minutes getting up his strength. Then with a great beating of his wings, he flew for the clouds as high as he could in one giant LOOP.

"What fun!" he exclaimed. "I'm never going to stop." But the second time he made his giant loop, he couldn't quite make it as high as he did the first time.

"What a shame," he buzzed. "I guess I'll have to use my swing flying technique instead of looping." So Bernard began SWINGING BACK AND FORTH, each time flying a little higher.

Soon he became so dizzy he had to stop. "There must be an easier way to fly the way birds do," he thought as he went swinging back and forth backwards, back to earth, the way he had come.

Whenever Bernard had a problem, he always took a little nap. As he told the other young bees, "Relaxing helps me think." And sure enough, by the time he had taken his nap, he had planned his next adventure.

"Watch me," he told his friends, "because this time I'm going to try high flying. That way I won't get dizzy!" So up he went to make a big SIDEWAYS LOOP like this . . .

"What a view!" he shouted.

Then he called down to his friends, "Hey down there, look at me! See how high I can fly!"

Bernard was inclined to show off a little, and while he did, his friends gathered in a big CIRCLE below to watch him.

Then Bernard did an even more daring sideways LOOP . . .

. . . and went almost as high as he had earlier that morning.

"I must go higher than any bee has ever gone," he whispered to himself. He was so pleased everyone was watching his amazing feats of flying.

Then Bernard made one mistake. He stopped for a moment and looked down . . . way down! His ROUND BEE HIVE looked very small from up so high.

Far below him he could see TWO of the same three BIRDS that he had seen that morning, but now he was so much higher in the sky, they looked much, much smaller than before.

Suddenly Bernard realized just how far above everyone he was. "Ooh," he shivered. "What am I doing up this high?"

That's when he decided to fly back to his hive as fast he could, but he was shaking and shivering so hard his wings wouldn't work right.

"Help! Help!" he called to his friends as he began to fall. When they saw he was having trouble flying, they ran and got a NET, hoping to catch him.

By this time Bernard was falling faster and faster, faster and faster. Where was the net? He missed it and landed "CRACK!" on his head.

Poor Bernard! Then and there he decided to stop showing off. And from that time on, he was the best behaved bee in his hive.

# THE LOST KEY

Joey and Will had been playing together all afternoon, but it was time for Joey to go home.

"Oh, no," he cried, as he looked in his pocket. "It's not here!"

"What's not?" asked Will.

"My house key," he moaned. "I must have lost it. Mom will really be mad if I can't find it. It's the second one I've lost this month!"

"Boy, you are in trouble," said Will. "Where do you think you lost it?"

"I don't know. It could be anywhere."

"Well, come on. We'll just have to go back to all the places we played this afternoon. Don't worry; we'll find it."

The first thing they did was to WALK AROUND Joey's house, but hard as they looked, they couldn't see his key.

"We were playing in your SANDBOX," said Will. "Let's look there." But still they found no key.

Will lived next door to Joey, so they went over to his house next. Slowly Joey CIRCLED the house . . .

. . . while Will looked around the swimming POOL.

"Any luck?" called Joey as he rounded the corner of the house.

"Not yet," yelled Will. "We'll just have to keep looking."

"What did we do after we went swimming?" asked Joey. "Oh, I know. We played ball at Henry's."

The boys walked AROUND Henry's house . . .

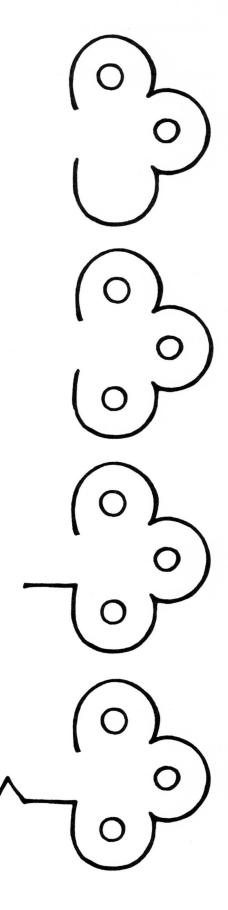

. . . but the only thing they found was the BALL they had used.

"Well," sighed Will, "the only other place we went today was to the park. We'd better search there." So OFF THEY WENT.

"Listen, Joey," said Will as they reached the park, "what we have to do is to remember everything we did this afternoon and keep our eyes open for your lost key."

"Okay," agreed Joey.

First they climbed UP THE SLIDE AND SLID DOWN.

Then they RAN to the monkey bars and SCRAMBLED ACROSS.

"Where did we go next?" asked Will.
"Ah, I don't know," responded Joey, "maybe on the see saw."
They RACED TO the see saw . . .

. . . and went UP AND DOWN.

"Gee, Will," said Joey, "we've done everything here, and I still don't
see my key. What'll we do now?"
"Let's go back," said Will.
So the boys TURNED AROUND AND RETRACED THEIR STEPS,
all the time looking for Joey's key.

Joey was really discouraged by the time they reached his house. He
knew how upset his parents would be. He jammed both hands into his
pockets, trying to think what he might do next.
"Oh, no!" he exclaimed. "I can't believe it!" He started jumping up
and down.
"What's the matter now?" asked Will.
"Matter? Matter? Nothing is the matter now," he said, pulling the
missing key from his pocket.
"Here it is! My key! I had it all the time. It was in my other pocket!"
The boys looked at each other and groaned. Then they started
laughing, and Joey hurried home to put the key in the lock.

# THE WATERSVILLE ZOO

"Can we, can we?" pleaded Nancy. "Please, can we go to the zoo?"

"You may if it's okay with Mrs. Delight," said her mother.

"Oh, I just know Mom won't care," said Carol.

"You'd better call and ask her though," advised Nancy's mother.

"All right," said Carol. A quick call and everything was arranged.

Before long the TWO GIRLS were standing in front of the main gate to the Watersville Zoo.

"I'll pick you up here at three o'clock," called Nancy's mother.

"We'll be right here at the gate," Nancy called back.

"This is really going to be fun!" exclaimed Carol.

"Sure is," said Nancy as they WALKED INTO THE ZOO.

As they walked through the gate, Carol motioned excitedly.

"Look, look over there," she said, pointing to a huge brown camel.

"Isn't he big!" said Nancy.

"And look at the TWO LARGE HUMPS on his back," said Carol.

"Is it true camels store water in their humps?" asked Nancy.

"That's what I read in a book," said Carol.

Next, the girls WALKED . . .

. . . over to the SEAL POOL.

"Look at them swim and dive," said Nancy.

"I sure wish I could swim that fast," said Carol.

"Now let's go over to see the polar bears next," said Nancy. "They're always fun to watch, too."

"Okay," agreed Carol. "Remember last summer when one of the mother bears had twin cubs?"

"Oh, yes! I wonder how big they've grown," said Nancy.

"Let's have a look," said Carol as they walked along the long CURVING PATH to the polar bear area.

When they arrived at the polar bear POOL, they saw that all the bears were fast asleep in the sun.

"Too bad they're all snoozing," said Nancy.
"Well," suggested Carol, "let's go on to the new Animal Mountain. We can come back when the bears are awake."
So they WALKED DOWN THE PATH leading to the new Animal Mountain.

On their way they passed a LARGE GOLDFISH POND.
"What beautiful fish," said Nancy.
"Yes, I've never seen goldfish so large," added Carol.

As they turned away from the goldfish pond, they caught their first glimpse of the new Animal Mountain. It was huge and had many animals on it. "Mountain goats!" exclaimed Carol. "I don't know how they ever manage to balance on those high rocks. Look at those TWO."
"It makes me scared just watching them," said Nancy.

Then both girls started laughing, because right in front of them one of the animals had poked it's head up and was staring right at them. While it watched them it ate a BANANA.

"Wouldn't you just love to take him home with us?" asked Carol. What kind of animal was it?

# PLANET Y

It was a history-making day at Space Command Headquarters. TWIN SPACESHIPS had just lifted off to go on a special mission . . .

. . . both headed for the same destination, the newly discovered PLANET Y.

The astronauts on board were very excited about their upcoming exploration of this planet, for scientists believed life could exist there.

"What kind of life do you suppose we'll find?" they kept asking one another.

Captain Williams said, "I'll bet my new ice cream machine that we only find plant life!"

"Oh, no," said Captain Robbins. "I'll bet my coin collection against your ice cream machine that we'll find life more like human beings."

Excitement mounted as the TV scanners picked up the PLANET.

"We're getting close now," reported the captains on their microphones.

A few minutes later the scanners picked up the path of Planet Y's MOON.

"Look at the speed of that orbit!" shouted Captain Robbins, for the moon was ORBITING AROUND THE PLANET very fast . . . like this.

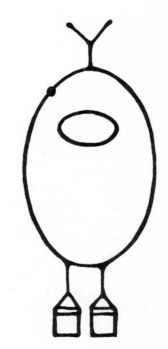

The spaceships FLEW CLOSER. "Prepare for landing," commanded both captains. Their crews became very busy for the next few minutes preparing to land.

Fortunately, both ships landed safely. One landed HERE . . .

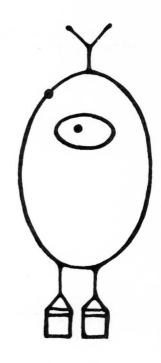

. . . and the other one THERE.

"Let's go outside and see what we can find," said the captains to their crews. "But be careful. We don't know what we might come across."

The two crews each went off in different directions, very excited and a little bit nervous, too. One group went off in THIS DIRECTION, shouting, "Good luck! See you back at the ships!"

The other group echoed, "Good luck!" and went off in THIS DIRECTION.

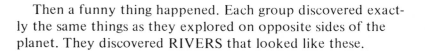

Then a funny thing happened. Each group discovered exactly the same things as they explored on opposite sides of the planet. They discovered RIVERS that looked like these.

And, as they inflated their boats and paddled down the rivers, they found that each river flowed into a large LAKE.

Captain Williams radioed to Captain Robbins, "I think we've had enough for today. Let's meet back at the ships."

"A-OK with me," responded Captain Robbins.

Both groups were disappointed, however, that they had seen no signs of any life on the planet, but they were hopeful some might appear the next day.

Then as Captain Robbins' group made their way back, one of the astronauts spotted something. "Look, look over there!" he called. "It must be a CAVE. Let's go in."

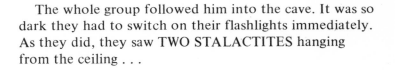

The whole group followed him into the cave. It was so dark they had to switch on their flashlights immediately. As they did, they saw TWO STALACTITES hanging from the ceiling . . .

. . . and a large STALAGMITE rising like a pillar from the floor of the cave.

"Oh, aren't they beautiful!" exclaimed Captain Robbins. "They're so . . ."

Just then he noticed a slight movement from behind the large stalagmite.

"Oh, my goodness!" he gasped, his voice trailing off in horror.

What the crew saw then made them all shudder! They rushed out of the cave as fast as they could and hurried back to tell the others what they had seen, exclaiming, "They'll never believe us. Never!"

What do you think they saw in the cave that was so scary?

# THE BIRTHDAY SURPRISE

"Happy birthday, sleepy head!" said Steve's mother as he came into the kitchen. "I thought you were going to sleep right through your birthday!"

"Oh, Mom," laughed Steve. "What time are the kids coming over for the party?"

"The invitations said two o'clock. Have you been in the living room yet?"

"No, why?"

"Well . . . there's something you might find interesting in there," said his mother with a twinkle in her eye.

Steve headed for the living room. "Terrific!" he shouted.

In the center of the living room sat a large wrapped PACKAGE.

"Can I open it?"

"Not until your party, young man," chuckled his dad as he looked up from his newspaper.

"Oh, please!" moaned Steve. "How can I ever wait?"

"Why don't you go outside and find something to do?" suggested his dad.

"All right," said Steve. He was really too excited to do anything else anyway, so he took a walk around the fence in their BACKYARD.

"Maybe there's something good on TV," he thought to himself. He went back inside and turned on the TELEVISION.

As he was watching a cartoon show, his parents came in carrying another package.

"Here, Steve," said his mother. "Before your friends arrive, we thought you might want to open this present your grandparents sent."

"Great!" shouted Steve. He flipped off the TV and began opening the present. "Oh boy . . . look at this," he said holding up a new BASKETBALL in one hand . . .

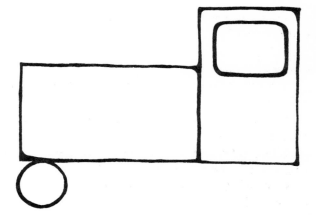

. . . and a basketball HOOP in the other.

"I wonder how Grandma and Grandpa knew what I wanted."

"Oh, somebody must have told them," said his mother as she gave his father a wink.

"And now I get to open the big package . . . right?" said Steve.

"Oh no you don't!" laughed his father. "You'll have to wait for that one!"

Fortunately, Steve didn't have long to wait, because at that moment his friends began arriving for his party.

"Here," said Steve's father handing out a PARTY HAT to each of Steve's friends. "Put one of these on and look at yourself in the mirror!"

They all put on their hats and laughed at how funny they looked. "And everyone gets a PARTY POPPER," added his father as he passed them out.

"What's a party-popper?" asked Steve's friend, Bill.

"Here, let me show you." Steve's father took one and gave its string a yank.

"Bang! ! !" went the popper, and different colored STREAMERS shot out the end.

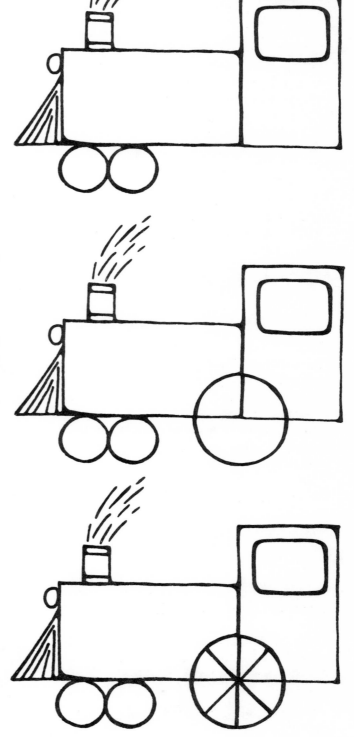

"Wow!" exclaimed everyone as they began shooting off their poppers. For the next few seconds all anyone could hear was laughing and the "Bang! Bang! Bang!" of party-poppers shooting into the air.

Then it was time for refreshments. Steve's mother opened the kitchen door and came in with a large round BIRTHDAY CAKE. She put it on the table, and everyone joined in singing "Happy Birthday."

When they had finished singing, Steve's mother cut the cake into EIGHT SLICES and served everyone a piece.

After they had all finished eating their cake, Steve looked at his parents with that certain special look.

"Okay," laughed his mom and dad. "Go ahead and open your present."

Steve could hardly wait. He ran to his present and ripped off the paper as fast as he could. Off came the box lid.

"Wow! Just what I wanted!" he exclaimed.

Can you guess what his present was?

# THE CAVE!

Troy and Mike were out exploring a new part of the forest behind Mike's father's farm.

"How far do you think we've walked today?" asked Mike.

"Oh, I'd say at least six miles," said Troy.

"Look over there," said Mike. "Those TWO LARGE ROCKS are just the place for us to eat our lunch."

"Hey, yeah, they're perfect!" replied Troy.

Just as the boys were sitting down on the rocks to have their lunch, Mike grabbed Troy's arm and whispered, "Look, over there, it's a bobcat!"

The boys jumped off the rocks and ducked under a bush. Off ran the bobcat, but the boys were in for an even bigger surprise.

"Look Troy! Look under here! There's a BIG HOLE in there."

It was a large hole all right . . . large enough for a boy to crawl through.

"Let's take a look inside," said Mike. "Maybe there's a treasure in there."

The boys began crawling under the bush into the hole.

"Wow!" exclaimed Troy.

"Hey, neat!" called Mike.

There was a LARGE CAVERN just ahead of them.

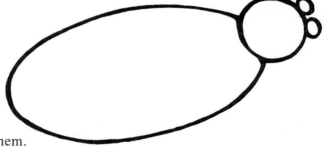

It was so dark the boys had to wait until their eyes adjusted to the dim light before they could go on.

"Do you think we should go in?"

"Well, we're already in!" said Mike. "But let's go just a little farther and have a good look."

The cave was so large that the boys could easily stand up. Slowly they WALKED FROM THE OPENING OF THE CAVE TO THE OTHER SIDE.

As they reached the wall of the cave, Troy tripped and fell.

"Ouch!" he yelled. His yell must have frightened some sleeping bats, because all at once the cave came alive with FLYING BATS.

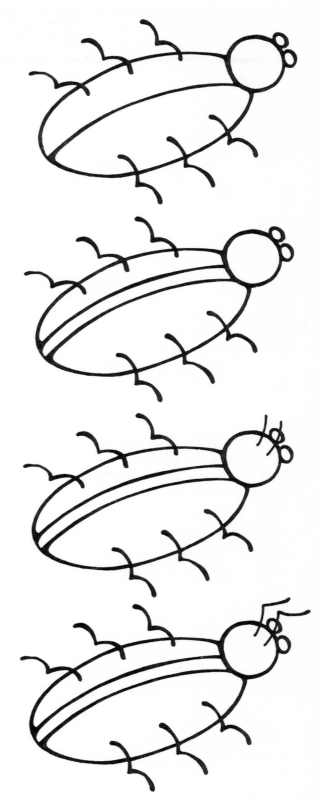

The boys squatted down in terror until the bats had gone back to rest.

"Boy, let's get out of here," whispered Troy.

"I'm with you," replied Mike.

Carefully and quietly they MADE THEIR WAY BACK TO THE OPENING.

They were almost out of the cave when they heard a strange scraping sound.

"I sure wish we hadn't come into this creepy cave," whispered Mike.

"Me, too!"

Just then something touched Mike's arm. He let out a yelp, and BOTH BOYS JUMPED UP . . .

. . . and CRAWLED OUT of the cave as fast as they could.

"Never again!" declared Troy. "That almost scared me to death."

"Me, too," added Mike. "I don't care if I never see a cave again."

Then they turned around and looked back at the dark opening of the cave. Their hearts were still pounding when they saw what had made them jump half out of their skin. Then they both started laughing as out of the cave came crawling a tiny . . .

What do you think had scared the boys?

# COVERED WITH RICHES

One day a young peasant boy was walking along a dirt ROAD to his village.

He was so poor he had no shoes, and the clothes he wore had been patched so often that there were patches over patches. As he walked FARTHER ALONG THE ROAD he became very thirsty, since it was a hot, dry day.

By and by he noticed an old WELL standing alone in the middle of a field.

"That's strange," he thought to himself. "I've been down this lane many times before, and I have never noticed that well." But since he was so thirsty, he thought no more about it and WENT STRAIGHT for the well.

As he dipped a bucket into the well, a strange voice surprised him. "Young peasant boy," called a voice from the well, "you have done many good deeds for others; now it is time you were rewarded."

"Who are you?" asked the boy as he looked down into the well.

"Never mind that," returned the voice. "Simply do as I say. You must go and find a scale from a lizard and bring it back to me. If you do this, I will see that you are covered with riches. Do you understand?"

"I guess so," stammered the peasant boy, "but where will I find a scale from a lizard?"

"That is for you to figure out. Now be gone!"

The peasant boy was puzzled, but he WENT DIRECTLY TO A HOUSE near the edge of his village.

The old woman who lived there thought he must be crazy, wanting a scale from a lizard. "Go away, silly boy," she shouted, and she took a swing at him with her broom.

The peasant boy scurried off. He WALKED DOWN THE PATH AND UP THE PATH until he came to the village. There he stopped at the first shop he saw.

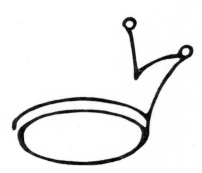

"Do you have the scale of a lizard?" the boy asked the shop-keeper.

"Certainly. I have twenty of them, you fool!" responded the shopkeeper, who then went about his work as if the boy were not there.

So the boy left and walked DOWN THE PATH AND UP THE PATH until he found a small park in the center of the village.

In the park he turned over many rocks looking for a lizard, but found not a one.

"I know," he thought to himself, "old Mrs. Wish will have one if anyone does." The people of the village whispered that old Mrs. Wish was really a witch because she did such strange things. So off he went DOWN THE PATH AND UP THE PATH to ask her.

Unfortunately, Mrs. Wish was not at home. He waited for her almost an hour; then decided to go DOWN THE PATH AND UP THE PATH to the river's edge. Surely he would find a lizard there!

As he reached the river's edge, a thought suddenly occurred to him. "That well is just teasing me. Lizards don't have scales!"

He was so angry that he went straight DOWN THE PATH and right back to the field where he had seen the well.

When he got there he stuck his head down the well. "Hello! Are you there?" he shouted in a voice loud and strong.

"Well, well, well," came back a small voice. "Have you brought me a scale from a lizard?"

"No, I have not," answered the boy mustering all the patience he could find. "I have not, and I did not because lizards don't have scales, and I do not think it was kind of you to send me on such a foolish errand."

"Well, well, well," came back the small voice again. "You have intelligence, spirit, and patience, as well as being a good boy. And to tell the truth, I was only testing you. Now if you will raise your head out of my well, you will find that you are covered with riches." And, indeed, the peasant boy was . . . for on his head that very moment he discovered . . . what do you think?

# WHO'S IN MY GARDEN?

Alexander lived in a little HOUSE far out in the country.

One spring day his mother said to him, "Alexander, how would you like a little garden all your own?"

"Boy, would I!" exclaimed Alexander. "Can I grow my own vegetables?"

"Sure can," said his mother, "but the first thing you have to do . . ."

"Oh, Mom, I know. I have to get some seeds."

"Right, so think about which vegetables you'd like to plant."

Alexander thought and thought and decided to plant his three most favorite vegetables. At the store he bought carrot seeds, corn seeds, and bean seeds.

When he got home, he showed them to his mother. "Look Mom, I've decided to plant three rows of each."

Out he went to begin spading the garden. Then he planted THREE ROWS OF CARROTS . . .

. . . and THREE ROWS of beans.

As he started to plant his corn, he discovered he had only enough seeds for two rows. Since he was in a hurry and wanted to go swimming with his friends that afternoon, he didn't get his ROWS OF CORN planted straight.

"Still," he thought, "I wanted more corn than this."

The next day his mother asked, "How about planting some flowers close to the back door? They'd be nice to look at all summer."

"Sure, Mom, glad to," said Alexander. So he planted a CURVED ROW of geraniums next to the house for her.

Alexander watched his garden closely every day. He was eager to see if his seeds would come up. It wasn't long before he saw rows of little plants peeking through the soil. His corn plants grew the fastest of all. It seemed like no time at all before he had TWO LARGE EARS OF CORN!

One morning when he went out to look at his garden, he saw something that made him very angry! Someone or something had been eating his vegetables. Many of the carrots and beans had been nibbled, but worst of all, TWO BIG BITES had been taken out of his ears of corn!

He showed them to his mother, but she had no idea what had chewed on his vegetables. "Why don't you build a fence around your garden?" she suggested.

"All right," said Alexander. "I'll try anything to save my vegetables."

So he built his FENCE. He enclosed all of his garden, but his corn was so tall that it towered high over the top of the fence.

The next morning he went out to inspect his garden, hoping nothing more had been eaten.

"Dog-gone!" he exclaimed disappointedly. Still more of his vegetables had been chewed away. He walked around the garden looking and looking. Then, near his corn plants, he discovered TWO HOLES.

He called his mother to have a look.

"Looks as if some animal is living in your garden, doing the damage," she said. "Why don't you try covering up the holes?"

So he took TWO LARGE ROCKS and pushed one down each hole.

"There," he said to his mother, "now my vegetables will be safe."

The next morning he awoke and ran out to his garden. Still more vegetables had been eaten! When he told his mother, she said, "Well, maybe there's another hole you haven't found yet. Why don't you go take another look."

Alexander looked and looked and looked some more, but never could find another HOLE . . . maybe because it was in the middle of the garden, and he was searching only around the edges.

He never discovered what was eating his vegetables. Can you guess what it was?

# TRICK-OR-TREAT

"What are you wearing tonight for trick-or-treat?" asked Ginny.

"I'm not telling," said Belinda. "I want it to be a surprise."

"Well, then, I'm going to surprise you, too," said Lynn.

"Me, too!" echoed Brenda.

The four girls were walking home from school. It had rained all afternoon, so they had to WEAVE IN AND OUT to dodge the puddles.

Before long they came to Belinda's house.

"I'll see you tonight," said Belinda as she hurried inside.

"Don't forget, six o'clock," the girls called back as they scattered for their own homes.

The girls were really looking forward to Halloween. They all hurried through their dinners and began putting on their costumes.

Ginny was the first one ready that night. She wore a witch's costume with a big ROUND HAT.

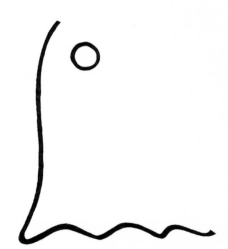

"Bye, Mom . . . bye Dad," she called out as she left.

"Bye, honey. Be careful," called back her mother.

She hurried TO LYNN'S HOUSE and rang the doorbell.

"Trick-or-treat!" she yelled. Lynn laughed, and Ginny did, too. "Oh, look at you, Lynn. You look so funny!"

Lynn had dressed like a clown with a big ROUND RED NOSE.

"Well, how about you!" laughed Lynn. "Where did you ever find that neat witch costume? It looks so real!"

"Mom made it for me. We had this old hat in our attic, but Mom made the rest of the costume."

"Do you have your trick-or-treat sack?" asked Lynn.

"Oh no!" moaned Ginny. "I was so excited, I forgot it!"

"That's all right," said Lynn's mother. She had just come to the door. "We have an extra one you can use."

"Gee, thanks, Mrs. Monday."

"Come on," said Lynn, "let's hurry to Brenda's. I can hardly wait to see how she's dressed."

"Me, too," said Ginny.

Brenda lived only two houses away, so it wasn't long before the girls had WALKED AROUND to her front porch.

"Trick-or-treat!" yelled Ginny and Lynn.

The front door of Brenda's house opened a crack, and a deep voice growled, "I am a ONE-EYED monster, and I am going to eat you up!"

"Wow!" said Ginny as Brenda pulled back the door and stepped out on the porch. "You look just awful with that one-eyed mask on."

"Yes," added Lynn, "you're going to scare the daylights out of people tonight."

"I'm sure going to try!" said Brenda.

"Well, here we go . . . a witch, a clown, and a one-eyed monster," said Ginny. "Let's get over to Belinda's house to see her costume."

The three headed DOWN THE SIDEWALK hurrying as fast as they could go in their costumes.

They walked up Belinda's driveway and were about to yell "trick-or-treat" when something jumped out from behind the shrubs and shrieked, "BOOOOOO!!!!!"

"Ahhhhhh!" screamed the girls as they jumped back.

"Ha, ha, ha!" laughed Belinda as she walked toward them. "I sure scared you."

"You sure did!" said Ginny.

"Look at you," said Brenda pointing at Belinda. "What a terrific costume!"

What was Belinda dressed up as?

# A THANKSGIVING FEAST

"Hurry up!" called Josh.

"I am hurrying," said Millie.

Josh and his sister raced up the path that lead to their CABIN.

"Last one in is a rotten egg!" yelled Josh as he ran through the doorway.

"That's not fair," panted Millie, as she followed him inside.

"What's not fair?" asked their mother.

"Oh, it's Josh," complained Millie. "He raced me to the cabin, but he had a head start!"

"Oh, such games you play," said Mrs. O'Leary. "Did you invite Little Horn and his family as I asked you to?"

"Yes'um," said Millie. "And they're coming!"

"Good," said Mrs. O'Leary.

This was going to be the O'Leary's first Thanksgiving on their new land. They had moved to the Ohio Valley early that spring. Now it was harvest time.

"Be careful of those Indians!" their friends in Pennsylvania had warned them when they began their journey west. But the O'Learys had found the Delaware Indians friendly, especially those who lived south of their land in THREE BARK-COVERED LODGES.

In honor of their friendship, the children had invited Little Horn and his family to their Thanksgiving dinner.

The O'Learys had worked hard that first spring and summer, and this first Thanksgiving was very special to all of them.

"Josh," said Mrs. O'Leary, "Go down to the river to fetch me some water in the pail."

"All right," said Josh as he started off. He was lucky the river ran so close to their cabin. He didn't have far to go. The river flowed past their cabin and CIRCLED around the Indian camp.

"Little Horn and his family said they'd be coming to our Thanksgiving dinner tomorrow," called Josh to his father as he LEFT FOR THE RIVER.

His father nodded. He was returning from the forest, his arms piled high with firewood for the next day. Millie and Josh stayed busy all that day helping their mother get ready for Thanksgiving.

The next morning they were up early. They could hardly wait for Little Horn and his family to arrive. Josh kept running down to the river to look for them. Finally, after at least his sixth trip to the riverbank, he saw their CANOE as it made the bend in the river.

"There they are!" he shouted.

"Hey, Little Horn. Happy Thanksgiving!" he yelled waving his arms. Little Horn raised his paddle in reply.

Little Horn, Josh, and Millie all had a great time. They played games, fished, and ate Thanksgiving food until they thought their stomachs would burst. Then, before Little Horn and his family went home, the men passed the peace pipe. While they smoked it as a sign of their friendship, the pipe SMOKE CURLED and drifted up around them.

Just then Millie came out of the cabin holding a gift for Little Horn. "I made this for you," she said handing it to him. His eyes grew large, and a smile lighted his face.

"Thank you," he said. "What do you call it?"

What do you think Millie had made for Little Horn?

# HAS ANYONE SEEN SANTA?

Darren was so excited that he just couldn't sleep. He had been in bed an hour already, but after all, it was Christmas Eve, and Santa would be coming . . . probably any minute. He crept out of bed and looked out through his small ROUND BEDROOM WINDOW.

First he looked up toward his ROOF to see if Santa's sleigh might be waiting for him there.

Then he looked across the sky and saw a very bright STAR, but still no sign of Santa!

"Oh, darn," he thought to himself. "I wish he'd hurry up and come. I can hardly wait!"

Next he looked down at the front yard. There inside the FENCE surrounding his yard he saw something.

"Maybe that's Santa," he whispered aloud. Then he remembered; it was only the SNOWMAN he had made the day before.

On the other side of their SIDEWALK . . .

. . . Darren saw their large EVERGREEN BUSH. "I wonder if Santa is hiding behind that?" he giggled. He tried to imagine Santa, the sleigh, and all the reindeer squeezed together behind that bush.

Just then he saw the lights go off at his friend's house across the street.
"I guess Jimmy has gone to bed," he murmured to himself. Then he had a terrible thought. "Maybe Santa won't come if I stay at the window and watch!"
He looked back at Jimmy's dark HOUSE . . .

. . . and hurried back to bed. He pulled the covers over his head and finally drifted off to sleep. He dreamed that Santa had come to his house and had brought a big, beautiful Christmas tree.
Do you think his dream came true?

# CAMPING OUT

Martha and Mary were good friends.  Here are their INITIALS.

One day they decided to camp out at CRANBERRY LAKE.

"Where shall we pitch out tents?" asked Martha when they
reached the lake.

"How about over there by the lake's edge?" suggested Mary.
"Then we can lie in our tents and fish at the same time."

"Great idea!" agreed Martha enthusiastically.  So both girls
pitched their TENTS next to the lake.

"Lets go swimming," called Mary from inside her tent.

"Okay!" said Martha. "But let's blow up the swim rings first so that we can float on them."

"Fine with me," Mary said as she began blowing up her swim ring.

When they finished blowing up their rings, they put on their swim suits, tossed their RINGS into the lake . . .

. . . and dove in after them. They swam under the water and came up IN THE CENTERS OF THEIR RINGS.

"Whew . . ." exclaimed Mary as she took in a big gulp of air and shook her head. "This water sure is cold!"

"Oh, it's not that cold," said Martha. "I'll race you to the center of the lake! That'll warm you up!"

"You're on!" shouted Mary as both girls began swimming as fast as they could.

They both REACHED THE CENTER of the lake at the same time.

"I won!" sputtered Mary.

"No, I did!" called Martha.

All at once a BOLT OF LIGHTNING and a loud crash of thunder silenced their arguing.

"Oh, no!" said Martha. "We'd better get back to our tents fast!"

As thay began swimming back another BOLT OF LIGHTNING came crashing down.

Then RAIN began to pelt the lake.

The girls scrambled up the shore and dashed into their tents.

"Yipes!" yelled Mary.

"What's the matter?" shouted Martha.

"Come here and look!"

The rain was pelting the canvas so hard that the girls could barely hear one another. Martha made a mad dash for Mary's tent.

"Gee!" exclaimed Martha. "How do you suppose it got in here?"

"I guess the lightning scared it in or it wanted to stay dry," suggested Mary.

What do you think was in Mary's tent?

# WHAT'S THAT SOUND?

Kevin pressed his nose against the window and muttered, "Rain, rain, rain. It's been raining all day."

"What did you say?" asked his mother, who was busy making donuts.

"That dog-gone rain . . . I was going fishing with Tim . . . but now there is nothing to do!"

"Why don't you play with one of your games or models?"

"Gee, Mom, I'm tired of doing the same old things all the time. It seems as if I've done everything."

"Now, Kevin," laughed his mother, "you couldn't have done everything! Look around, and I'm sure you'll find <u>something</u> new to do."

Kevin shook his head. "No, there's just nothing new to do."

"Here," said his mom, "help me make these DONUTS."

"Aw, Mom, . . . I don't want to do <u>that</u>," said Kevin. He left the kitchen and WALKED into the dining room.

He looked out the dining room window again, but all he saw was rain, rain, rain! "What luck," he complained to himself. "All my plans are spoiled. Well, maybe I can find something to do in my room." He WALKED down the hall . . .

. . . and opened the DOOR.

Then he went slowly AROUND his room looking for something to do . . .

. . . but all he found half interesting was a puzzle. "Well," he thought, "maybe a puzzle is better than nothing." He DUMPED OUT the puzzle the floor.

After a few minutes putting his puzzle together, he got up. "Good grief!" he thought. "There must be something better than this. I know, I'll look in the attic. Maybe I'll find something to do there."
So UP to the attic he went.

The first thing he saw in the attic was a big trunk with a lot of clothes in it. Right on top was one of his old CAPS . . . one he'd worn when he was a baby.

He tried it on his head, just for fun. It certainly was small. Then he started looking at other things . . . when suddenly he heard a strange, high sound. It seemed to be coming from downstairs.

"What could that be?" he thought. "I'd better go see if Mom needs help!" He hurried DOWN to the kitchen . . . as the sound grew louder and louder.

As he hurried through the dining room, he noticed the rain had stopped and the sun was shining.

"Kevin, is that you?" called his mom. "Come look at the beautiful RAINBOW."

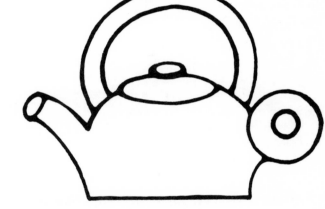

Kevin could see it out the window as he entered the kitchen. It was a beauty.

His mom was seated at the kitchen window with a plate of donuts in front of her.

"Sit down, Kevin. We're going to have donuts and hot spiced tea . . . just the thing for the end of a rainy day."

Then Kevin realized where the strange sound had been coming from. It was the whistling of their teakettle. It had stopped the minute his mother had taken it off the stove!

"Well," admitted Kevin, "at least something happened on this rainy day that I didn't expect."

He sat down to enjoy his donuts and tea . . . and they were very good.

# WHAT'S SO IMPORTANT?

"Get up, sleepy-head!" called Billy's sister. "The sun is shining. It's a perfect day."

"Oh, do I have to?" yawned Billy as he pulled the covers over his head. "Why do I have to get up?"

"Because I have something very important to do today. Mom is going to take me, and you get to go along. So hurry up and get ready."

"Hummm . . . " thought Billy to himself as he CRAWLED out of bed. "I wonder what's so important."

He put on his bathrobe and WALKED DOWN THE HALL to the kitchen. The room smelled of good things his mom was fixing for breakfast.

"Morning, Billy. How many eggs do you want for breakfast?"

"Morning, Mom. I'm hungry. How about a dozen?"

His mom laughed. "How about if we start with two. You can have more later if you're still hungry." She stepped OVER TO THE STOVE and dropped two eggs into the frying pan.

"Mom, what's Cindy in such a big hurry for this morning?"

"That's for me to know and you to find out," broke in Cindy as she CAME RACING THROUGH the kitchen door. "Don't tell him, Mom."

"Oh, so it's a big secret, is it? Cindy, please get the plates out of the cupboard and bring them here."

Cindy REACHED FOR THE PLATES. They were on the top shelf and rather hard to get down.

She placed them on the counter next to her mom; then WENT OVER AND SAT DOWN with Billy.

"Come on, Cindy," pleaded Billy. "What are you up to today?"

"Oh, just something special," she said with a mysterious smile.

"Chow's on," said his mom handing them each a plate. On Billy's plate were TWO BIG EGGS cooked sunny side up, just the way he liked them.

His mom WENT BACK TO THE SINK to rinse a pan.

"How about bacon, Mom?" asked Billy.

"Coming right up." She brought over TWO LONG, THIN SLICES and put them on his plate between the two eggs.

"Come on, Cindy. Won't you even give me a hint?"

"Well, maybe just one," she said as she WENT TO THE REFRIGERATOR to get milk for everyone.

"I'm going to be washing something today to earn money for my girl scout troop. You get to help, and afterward I'll treat you to an ice cream soda."

Billy thought a moment. Then he JUMPED UP from the table. "I know!"

Can you guess what Cindy's girl scout troop was going to wash?

# WHAT ARE YOU MAKING, GRANDPA?

"Be careful crossing the streets," called Mrs. Robby. "I will," said Ted.

"And don't forget to say 'Hi' to grandma and grandpa for me."

"I won't."

Ted was going to visit his grandparents. They lived only five blocks away, so he went often to see them.

"I don't know why Mom worries so much," he thought to himself as he crossed Washington Street. He turned down Vermont Avenue and headed for his grandparents' small red HOUSE.

When he was nearly there, he saw his grandmother waving to him from the kitchen WINDOW.

"Oh, boy," he thought. "I hope she's making cookies. They're so good hot out of the oven." He raced into the house.

"Hi, Grandma."

"Hi, honey. I bet I know what you want."

Ted grinned. "Sure do love your cookies, Grandma. Do you have any left?"

"They're in baking," laughed his grandmother. She gave him a hug. "I'll let you know as soon as the first batch comes out of the oven."

"Good. Where's Grandpa?"

"Out in the workshop. He's waiting for you. Go on out to see him."

Grandfather's WORKSHOP was in an old barn behind the house. He had lots of tools there and plenty of space to work.

Ted went out the back door and RACED DOWN to the workshop.

"Hi, Grandpa!"

"Hi, Ted."

Grandfather was leaning over his workbench. "How's your mother?"

"She said to say, 'Hi,' Grandpa. What are you making?"

"Oh, it's a surprise!" he said, taking a saw and cutting through a long board.

"Grandpa, how do you know which saw to use?"

His grandfather held up his saw. "See these TEETH? Well . . . they're larger than the teeth on my other saw, so they can cut this big board faster."

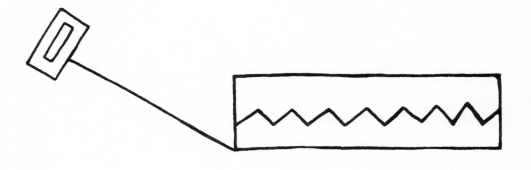

Before long Ted's grandmother brought her cookies DOWN TO the workshop.

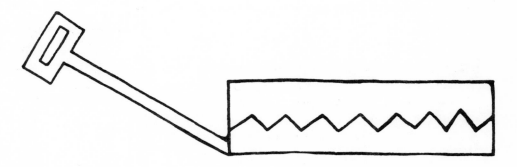

"Here they are . . . hot from the oven," she said. She handed
one PLATEFUL to Ted . . .

. . . and another PLATEFUL to his grandfather.

"Oh, Grandma, they're my favorite kind."
"I wouldn't think of making any other kind
for you, honey. You love sugar cookies just as
your mother did . . . with one big RAISIN right
in the middle of each cookie."

"Grandma," asked Ted, "do you know what
Grandpa is making?"
"I think it's a surprise, honey. I think it's
something you'll like."
Can you guess what Ted's grandfather was
making for him?